T0063356

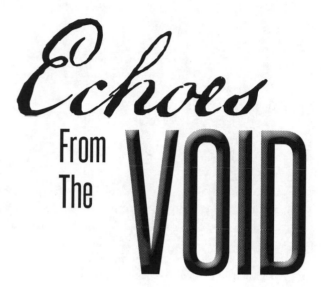

# ROBERT HALSEY

PARTRIDGE
A Penguin Random House Company

Copyright © 2014 by Robert Halsey.

| ISBN: | Softcover | 978-1-4828-9845-3 |
|---|---|---|
| | eBook | 978-1-4828-9861-3 |

All rights reserved. No part of this book may be used or reproduced by any means, graphic, electronic, or mechanical, including photocopying, recording, taping or by any information storage retrieval system without the written permission of the publisher except in the case of brief quotations embodied in critical articles and reviews.

Because of the dynamic nature of the Internet, any web addresses or links contained in this book may have changed since publication and may no longer be valid. The views expressed in this work are solely those of the author and do not necessarily reflect the views of the publisher, and the publisher hereby disclaims any responsibility for them.

**To order additional copies of this book, contact**
Toll Free 800 101 2657 (Singapore)
Toll Free 1 800 81 7340 (Malaysia)
orders.singapore@partridgepublishing.com

www.partridgepublishing.com/singapore

# Preface

Our beliefs and values have been accumulated over many years as we have grown up and matured or failed to do so.

These beliefs and values have come to us through what we have heard, seen or witnessed and have critically assessed and assimilated or have failed to do so.

Nothing is ever really expunged or utterly forgotten but keep returning to us from time to time like echoes from a distant, or not quite so distant past, or void. I use the word "void" not as absence of everything but as the fertile breeding ground of values and beliefs that lurk around waiting as it were to be reassessed and which enrich, or enhance more connotational meaning to emerging beliefs.

We come alive in an inner environment only by constantly questioning, or being open to other views that fertilise one's own. One begins to question only by being awake, thinking and doubting or at least challenging those thoughts that come to us. It really does not matter who or what it is that we question and challenge. There is a cathartic effect that produces what we can absorb, reasonably accept as being true. It leaves no room for lazy thinking, much less for superstitious thought or mythology that has derived from very conservative and erroneous meanings of another generation that lacks the energy to engage.

There are those who agree with what I have just said but choose nevertheless do nothing about it because it may prove to disadvantage their status or escape the accusation of hubris. At best they resort to rationalize and compromise. Their position is always a clinging to a priori values and beliefs. They feel, or hope, the traditional is inviolable; whatever is in the Book is right. I once heard Richard Holloway say that it was strange that some people choose to prove the truth of a book by the truth of the doctrines or creeds it contains and at the same time insist the doctrines and creeds to be true by being in that book.

I don't propose to my reader that I am correct and everyone else is wrong. Just the same, I am put upon when I come across in a discussion those who humor me and always hold the traditional values and beliefs, whatever they may be and however they may have been derived, as being God-given. For them all has been signed, sealed and delivered. There can be no room for doubt, no room for the new. They leave no room for growth.

Doubt, for me, derives from what I hear as echoes that come welling up from the deepest part of my being. It represents at looking at some beliefs again It must be the same for everyone. It may come unbidden, inspired, derived from a sudden insight as one reads a book or listens to a speaker, or a relationship. Often one is not prepared to deal with it just then or in the future, or able to. This may be an outcome that arrives accompanied by fear of some consequences. Or it could be lazy thinking.

Often echoes swirl about and may even be absorbed into some nascent and challenging idea. This is an evolutionary growth that anyone should be happy about as it shows that one is alive and not with the albatross of dead creeds and dogmas killing you off slowly till there is nothing left of spirituality and there is nothing to be done but go through the usual, inherited practices in a sort of spiritual somnambulism chanting tired mantras of the past.

So, my dear reader, what I offer you are no daring, and new, ingenious theologies or offer of peace with yourself. "Echoes" is only the musings of merely one man, a record of what has occurred in me, a mere process, as it were. We Unitarians are known to say, "We have no answers, only questions."

Robert Halsey

Bibra Lake 2013

# *Foreword*

As a priest, I often think that my most important job is to tell the truth. Even when the truth is not particularly comfortable, and even when it challenges familiar and well-worn mental or spiritual habits. My personal feeling is that hearing and owning the truth—about ourselves, and about the world around us, and about God—while it can be unnerving and even disorientating at first—in the long run helps us to see clearly, to give of ourselves whole-heartedly and to love and be loved without pretence.

As a priest it is sometimes not easy to tell the truth, especially when for so many of us religion seems to function as a comfy cushion, something squishy to insulate us against the hard edges and cold surfaces of life. This sort of religion keeps us 'nice' (at least that's the theory), gives us a set of rules that most of the time ensure we get along with others, and a reason not to ask too many hard questions. I don't subscribe to squishy religion, not because I have a puritanical streak that demands nothing, not even religion, should be comfy, but because I think squishy religion, when it comes down to it, isn't very helpful. Living your life with an internal map cobbled together out of half-remembered Sunday school stories and undigested dogmas that take the place of honest observations and open-ended questions and wonder is not, when it comes down to it, the adult option. And I don't believe squishy religion serves us well when life takes us through hard places, negotiating our own personal morass of joy and heartache, desire and regret until, at the last, we face the great question-mark of our mortality.

Atheism, incidentally, is a particularly squishy sort of religion, for all that its adherents solemnly assure us that as the 'brights' they see clearly the nothingness at the heart of everything that everybody else has missed. Because atheism, when it comes down to it, is not particularly observant, it fails to see the deep-down 'is'-ness of things and it doesn't ask very hard questions, for example about what human life means and why it matters. It fails as a result to see the poignancy in its effort to deny death by pretending, in effect, that we were never alive in the first place. Atheism sends us all shopping, which when it comes down to it is only marginally more helpful than hard pews and the singing of hymns. If your particular brand of religion—or non-religion—doesn't leave you open-mouthed with wonder and with way more questions than answers, then personally I think you're missing out on the ride of your life.

Preaching, for priests who want to tell the truth, is not always easy. Not because of squeamishness about spilling the secret that, quite possibly, Jesus didn't walk on water or feed a crowd of five thousand with a little boy's play-lunch. I have always found congregations of normal adult Anglicans quite happy to concede that God might not make a habit of arbitrarily suspending the laws of physics just to impress us (or by way of insisting that we believe in the clearly silly and impossible, in order to make sure that only the credulous and unintelligent make it to heaven?). Maybe I just haven't served the right congregations, but mine do seem prepared to go with me on this, that oral traditions evolve in ways that accentuate the colourful, that ancient texts and authors use different conventions than modern ones but that doesn't mean they're lying, and that rather than getting hung up on literalism we might instead think about what the stories are actually saying. Which is that in the prophet, Jesus of Nazareth, we see the creating and sustaining Wisdom of God at work.

But telling the truth in sermons is hard nonetheless, because the truth that is hardest to face is not so much the truth about stories in the Bible, as the truth about the stories we tell ourselves. Jesus was great at telling the truth to the people he encountered, and that's my job too, as a priest.

Anyway I think it was one Sunday morning over coffee and a squishy Swiss roll that a fine lady in my congregation with a great sense of humour looked at me quizzically and said, 'You might like my brother-in-law. He's written a book.'

That book was *Voices from the Void*. *Echoes* is its sequel. The void is the creatable darkness of God, in which we have our beginning and our true end—though one suspects that for Rob, the end is a new beginning. Rob keeps up a running conversation with the void in such a way that you know he understands it runs right through him—that if in a sense the void is his making and unmaking then it is also the companionate murmur that he hears in the ticking of his heart and the soft whoosh of his breath. The void is the energy that crackles everything to life and the memory that is all that's left of us as we pass. Maybe it sounds solipsistic but it isn't—Rob's sometimes cranky sometimes querulous interrogation and the void's maddening silence in return leaves us in no doubt that what is being celebrated here is a lifetime of love that endures—not in spite of corns and the aching of octogenarian joints but maybe because of them and best articulated through their familiar lexicon of senescence. The void, in other words, is definitely Other, a most intimate if demanding lover.

Rob is truthful, which of course is not to say that he is always right. He carefully skirts just the wrong side of orthodoxy, and I believe has a lot of fun doing it. Which brings me to my second hobby horse, the joy of being wrong. Whatever gave earnest pastors and theologians the idea that God expects them to be right all the time? Not loving may very well cause God some grief, not having a sense of humour most definitely, but using your brain to its full capacity and managing to draw different conclusions from the doctors of the Church must at the very least gain us marks for trying. Be as wrong as you feel like, be heartily and muddle-headedly wrong—God delights in your capacity to reason and speculate and wonder and in your wrong turns as well—but even more so when we can disagree with one another happily, with affection and respect.

I agree with a lot of what Rob says, and I hope you do too. I love the delight he has in words. He admirably fulfils the poet's brief of putting the flesh of intuition and beauty on the intricate dry bones of process metaphysics. I love his implicit assumption that creation is where it's at, not some distant hypothetical heaven, and his intuition that all there really is, is now. I try not to get too defensive when he has a go at clergy and the Church, because heaven only knows we can use a bit of ginger. I respectfully disagree with his conclusion that the sacraments of the Church have lost their zing: their power, that is, to deconstruct and transform us, and to open us to the beauty of what is. As a medievalist, I have a healthy respect for the wisdom of ancient thinkers, and I have tried to suggest to Rob that not all his ideas are necessarily shocking or even new. He takes this with good humour, and I hope he indulges me with many more debates.

Rob's work is important because it is true, because he faithfully charts the course of his soul and closely observes the world around him; and because he understands that science and religion, treated properly, both lead to humility and wonder. He goes round in circles, sometimes, because that's the direction life takes us. Sometimes he appears to doubt himself, to wonder whether, after all, he might not have wasted his time. This is a mark, I suggest, of authenticity. If you need a deep clear lungful of eternity, a glimpse of what's within and beyond and beneath you, then take the phone off the hook and switch off the telly tonight, because this one is for you.

Fr Evan Pederick,
St Michael and All Angels Anglican Church, Cannington
evan.pederick@perth.anglican.org

# Echoes From The Void

Those on whose tongue falls a drop of rain
Long to drink the ocean.

There is an end,
but not the end
of us who will be transformed
and for whom there is no end.
Everything in history
comes to an end,
but not they
for whom history wasn't written.
Empires die and fade away.

I grow more aware
of making my way towards
my coming change of being.
I find the weights and sounds
of words I need
to say what needs to be said
resist the will to get it said.

In the quietness of my room
I lie in wait for a language
of what's beyond it all
to speak to me
about what I really believe,
but which evades my conscious efforts.
The searchings of my heart
are like a foreign language
I think I once knew,
but have long since lost
through the passage of years.
Welling up from the void
I catch the sound of words
that bring life to what I feel,
and, feeling, know
but I feel I am not equipped
to use before they dance away.

Inspiration brings with it a light
that is often too bright
and lasts only the life time of the flash.
It may show but does not reveal,
being intrusively transcendent
and just as evanescent.

As the act of making known
ends too soon,
it leaves me incomplete,
alienated in a wordless life,
ever so near but just as far away.
Where and what it touched
reverberates like a fading echo
that will not let me rest.

I am too deeply seized
by my existence,
too webbed in instinct and emotion
to read more clearly
what's revealed,
as little as that may be,
and as I seek to identify them
I find myself picking through
the trash bins of old ideas
that once excited me,
as the old metaphors once did.
I know the anguish and the crush
of incoherence
and the heaviness of loss.
Whatever follows from the lightning flare,
enfeebled as it becomes,
feeds the creative urge
and teases out the life of words
that I regard as a reproach to life.

Answers change: questions don't.
It takes courage to confront self-delusion
and investigate safe and pleasant
culturally sanctioned ideas
one may be at odds with.
The intuitive pulse throbs,
inner perceptions
rouse us to make
the unseen, unknown visible
and bring some little clarity to the ineffable
and the eternal question:
What is the what?

I awaken some nights
to the haunting
of ghosts of loss
of a past faith
and words that once warmed me
with comforting beliefs
I now deem delusional.
Creeds now dead and cold
lie like ashes where no embers live.

I now think how strange
comfort can be found
in the strangest places
like pulpits and play pens.

The hour is late.
Hours of darkness
fail to conceal
a gnawing hunger
that feeds the urgency alive,
between heart, mind and being.

Echoes in empty churches
of long-enduring prayers
and snatches of fading
and singing of all
but forgotten hymns
rising with the fragrance
of incense and candle-wax.
Memory blurs and fades
what faith can no longer reveal,
what's not there any more.
Today's devotees are like
the children of lost Israel
meandering in the desert,
led by a crazy tour guide
who had long lost his
global positioning system,
hence had now lost his way
and now his use-by-date,
wild-eyed and of doubtful sanity,
shouting into sandy wastes of desert.

Old limits have long been breached.
What has waited all these years,
always just beyond knowing,
but merciless and uncompromising
in its challenge to us today,
calls from the deepest depths
of an implacable Being.

The past is now another country
like ours, full of parched fields,
empty lakes, empty water courses
and burnt trees bleached of colour.
What was once its music
is now all electronic noise
rising in swirling, fading echoes—

I must trust what now emerges
rising out from mists of doubt:
silence feeds my search for belonging
to a sense of a living presence
that promises a seamless flow
into the Oneness
that embraces all my
yesterdays, todays and tomorrows.

The breath of dawn
returns to earth
the colours the darkness stole.
So, too, is my faith restored
when silence flows from out of
distant truths
not all of which can ever be
wholly known but rather deep down felt.
Just as spring rain
softens the earth with renewed life
so, too, my faith comes alive
with surprised and welcome peace.

I shall not fear my demon doubts.
Let me offer hospitality
to all those I needs must have
because I cannot keep them out.

Worthwhile life begins
when I am claimed
by urgencies that fill my world,
but go unheeded and ignored:
they aren't all understood.
What I cannot know
silently clamours
like echoes that come from
beyond distant stars
and giant suns
that awaken my sluggish pulse
and run along every fibre of my body.
I come to know I am not alone.
It makes me feel your belonging
in the Oneness of it all,
just as it always has
and will be ever more.

Life has no meaning, I feel, except
in the mystery of chance and randomness
of the evolving God
who is constantly coming into Being
in ways beyond our knowing.
This larger meaning encompasses
us all and will absorb us all
when we no more move here on earth,
as we, too keep coming into being
in a God who doesn't have to be understood.

Do we make too much of this earthly life?
Look up at the stars,
feel at one with all
and deeply breathe.

Something exists instead of nothing
and no one knows why.
We look for answers everywhere
because that's the way we are.

Are these questions about God
being asked on distant planets,
in other worlds
four hundred billion worlds away?

There are always different answers
but the questions remain the same.

You've lived in human consciousness,
my God, but will you for, no longer
than the blink of an eye,
die away when
this constellation implodes
and returns to cosmic dust again?
These echoes are struggling
In my spiritual cyber space.
You and all that comprise you,
in this life,
are the sustaining mystery,
the You who is in search
of the Being that keeps evolving anew.

Whoever seeks to know you
asks for proof.
Practitioners of reason
seek you for their creeds.
You are ruarch.
No one knows from where it comes,
no one knows where it goes,
or how we can track it,
but we feel it just the same.

No change can ever come
without the diminution
or the ending of the old.
All we build or achieve,
our desires, hopes or needs,
are all short-lived.
The dying who pray to live
will live to die another day.
Death must come sooner or later.
And so death is felt and feared
because we fail to realize
birth never comes without pain.
Death is a part of life.
We human beings don't do too well
Handling the sacred paradoxes.
There is hope beyond every sadness
as we evolve in and with our God
in whom we are embedded.
In this subdued and somber joy
there is an all-consuming awe.
In this awe let us, then, build our faith.

We are made of star stuff.
We are brought to life
by the energy that flows
through the universe,
and when this phase of being passes
we are returned into
the evolving process,
like galaxies dying and being born again.
Becoming never ends.
Let us celebrate this hour, this day,
celebrate our consciousness
which permeates our life and being
and which sets us apart
from the rest of the cosmos,
as far as we can tell, for now.

To pray is to be still
and at peace with and in God
and ourselves
in a sacred unity
which is the center of life.

It is then that we are at our fullest,
in the center of our mystery,
breathing in and with God.

So now you know, my God,
what it's like to be human,
after millions of years of monkey tricks.
I wonder what you'll be like
another million years from now.
Whatever it may be
it won't be here on Earth.
But for now you've learnt what fear is,
what pain, hunger and thirst are,
what beauty, joy and love,
faith and love are.
And not to give a damn, any way.

Long past the chatter of apes
you now listen to the chatter of men
and what we make of you
and tell you what you are
in our symbols and metaphors
drawn from human experience
that grace the many weird
and wonderful tales and prayers,
creeds and dogmas.
You know what you've discovered
in the many relationships
born out of sexuality
and the randomness of chance.
Does it make you smile?

If it wasn't for us,
would this part of you
in your coming into Being
be incomplete
Without self-realisation?

Songs of the ocean
rise from whales and dolphins;
cadences from the air
are carried out by the caroling of birds.
You hear the vespers of viruses
and the music of the microbes.
You come alive in the anthem of life
till all the sounds fade away in whispers
as the silence of the dark hole
when the curtain falls,
and life that awaits the phoenix hour
renews the surge into another being
into time of another time
and the Being outside of being.

I'm not sure we really know
what life is.
I carry millions of life forms,
germs, bacteria and viruses
in and on my body
and full of electrical energies
that resonate with all those which surround us—
I do not know how or why.

Man is 98% bacteria they say.
Some I'll kill so that I may live.
There are those which will kill me some day.
It's kill or be killed.
What is the purpose of this life?
Here is the persistent paradoxical conundrum again.
It is never far away.

If I am even 80% bacteria, my God,
what does that make you?
Does that make you super-bug?
Just what am I to make of all this?
How and why did all this get started
leaves us all bewildered.
But that is just the way it is,
All of the one substance,
as it was, is now and ever more will be.

Four hundred billion worlds were born
in the twinkling of an eye,
born in cosmic fire,
and you exploded into Being.
Space cooled.
Photons, quarks, neutrinos
began to appear
giving shape
to your body immaterial.
One billion years later
matter began to form,
shaping stars, galaxies and man.
Bacteria once offered the only life you had,
oh my bacteria-born God,
now cherished by
your bacteria-riddled people.
I wonder if we haven't got all this wrong.

Science whispers to my soul,
"Hold fast, my cowering one.
Faith doesn't live in certainties.
You have a right to be wrong
even when you know you're right."

We have been called chemical scum.
What an original thought—scum!
Someone doesn't love us, I guess.
But what does that make you, my God?
The catalyst that brings about all things new
in a changeless process?
All the isotopes, radiation and nuclear energies
blend into coherence
that produces love, beauty, reason,
and the conundrum found
in form and diversity,
and all the while
you seem to smile,
drifting away from immediate reality
towards where you have to go and be.
You have no control
how you are to be
because that is just how you
are and how you have to be.

Lost amidst millions of stars and suns,
infinitesimally small and lost
to worlds unseen and as yet unknown,
the caterpillar yields its short life
to a leafy grave.
It enters its mausoleum life,
into its intermediate chrysalis world,
hard-shelled against intrusions
of traditions and past creeds,
sure that everything is lost and past
to growing and congealing darkness.
Sure that all is lost, life is over,
it suddenly becomes a butterfly
and flies into the sudden
aching and bursting light of the sun,
into a new life, into a new world,
alive in its meaning,
and its process-living
in a new time, in a new world.

We need to talk about butterflies,
talk about time and outside time,
to talk about be-ing
outside of self and ego.

They say my thoughts
are cold and too remote.
No mention of love, joy and hope.
There's nothing about God the Father
or about our Maker, Protector and Provider
to whom we owe our daily bread.
We can play these games—
(ask any horse and he'll tell you God is a horse!)—
and make him what we will
but it's always in our own image
and then we stick him in our creeds
for control and power.
We end up with the worship of the Church
and forget about God.
Let me tell you once more, my friends,
There is no God but God,
neither Creator nor Creation.
There is only God,
the Nameless One,
the Unknowable One,
the Ultimate Reality,
The sacred Infinity
In which we are engulfed
as a part of God,
in God, but uncreated.

Your dark mystery
is our absurdity,
which is why there are
so many versions of you,
and why some choose
to deny that you exist.
Some have entered
the world of the absurd
where they think you are to be found.
Not in reason but in humility and love
that evoke awe and peace,
we should worship you,
not in audible metaphors
nor in chanting doxologies
no matter how they may appeal to us,
not in conceptual abstractions
but in the quietness
and stillness of the heart.

I've got to go, it's late.
Shut the book,
turn off the computer
and put off the light.
The more I lose myself
In the lonely stretches of cyber space
listening, letting silence seal me in,
the loneliness spreads through me.
I feel it's a loneliness you share.
You've looked through our eyes
ever since we evolved
as thinking beings.
You couldn't have done this before
four million years ago.
What did you do in those
un-peopled times
and early homo sapiens time,
how did you get on with Lucy?
For us it's getting too late already.
Come into your fullest self, O God.
That's where we want to be,
redeemed and perfected
in you and you in us.

I shouldn't have to look for a place
to talk with you, my God.
Speak to me from everywhere,
in every thing that comes my way.
The mind sets its own limitations.
It behaves like a tourist,
here, there and everywhere.
It takes us all over the place,
without getting us anywhere.
We are tired and distracted.
When we go to you, my God,
we need to go entire,
whole and committed,
clear in mind and spirit.

I believe in my darkness,
the darkness that embraces everything,
worlds far and near.
It is from where we come.
It is where everything begins and ends.
The Void is never emptiness
but anything and everything to be,
nothing with shape and definition
but gestational and embryonic,
potential and promise
of what is yet to be,
born out of chance and risk,
struggling towards the end,
resisting chaos and decline
but building on what has been,
of all that was once glitter and gold,
now nothing but gross and mould,
out-moded and irrelevant
as darkness swallows everything.
It is there that we are emergent
embraced in One-ness,
renewed, restored and re-defined.
Let me feel your warm embrace
and your spirit flowing through me
to energise my faith in you,
and from this self set free
to become what and where I should be.

How can I trust you, my God,
trust what you've revealed to me,
or trust what I think you have made to me
or trust what I may have made of you?
You've never been the same.
We like you have changed so much down the years.
How much someone must have loved you
and wanted everyone to love you, too.
Or, how fearful you appeared to someone
who wanted desperately to warn others, too.
Some others claim they can manage both,
fear and love you with a sort of fearful love.
Now suddenly there you are—
in the outer reaches of the universe
and in the closet corners of our selves
yet in the heart of everything.
Why must we load you
with every human emotion?
Are you really hungry for our love,
humility and fear?
It occurs to me to ask you, oh God,
"Why did you create us? Did we have to be?"
I sometimes wonder if it matters to you
whether we love you or not,
or whether we can believe
in what we make of you.
Your darkness is darker
than the darkness that you are,
than what it should mean
to all of us who still look for you.

The prophets of old
have passed away;
so too have soothsayers,
readers of tea leaves!
(though sometimes I wonder)
those who tell the future
consulting stars and crystal ball,
and those who dress in surplices
and still practice their comic art.

The prophets of the Second Axial Age,
prophets of today and tomorrow
are white-coated scientists
at the cutting edge of research.
They proclaim their gospels
bringing the good news.

They peel back veil after veil
that hides you from us.
They take the search for the living truth
deep as they can to distant worlds,
the millions that lie around
the growing, expanding universe.
They take us the deepest we have ever been
into our wondering but adoring souls.
They now know, as so should we,
that the universe is alive within.
In everything and everywhere
we see the Unity in and of all things
expressed in radiant, transcendent
communion within community.

Throughout this universe and beyond
God keeps coming into Being.
We see it in terms of birth and death.
We see stars dying and bursting into life.
It takes death to bring forth life.
The sun that gives us life
will be our grave when it dies,
and in dying will spew forth new life.
Today Betelgeuse, tomorrow some other.
Every part that I think is you
was once a part of something else.
Dear God, lead us to ask the questions
we need to find ourselves and
where it is that we belong.
We know we can never know you.
All we ask is to feel you move within us.

I watched the caterpillar
eat and leave
what remained of a red geranium.

I watched what I thought
was a predator
but all I saw
was my predator
measure its last moments in the sun
as it approached its end.

Denied its beautiful gossamer wings
it might have had,
it made its last green lurch,
unsuspecting, but strangely forgiven
as I sensed a sharing
of the inch by inch
going into where we all have to go.

I see the ocean heaving
white-crested
waves upon the shore.

I see mottled fish flashing
red and gold
suddenly disappear into the deep,
its watery world
growing bitter every day.

I see the eagle
in gallant flight
search out poisoned thermal currents
to carry it to safer height,
but only for a while,
for return to earth it must.

I looked for my shadow
but it had gone,
melting into shadowless light
that swallowed everything alike.

Between first light and last
is all a motion
that impels all things forward,
half-perceived,
between thought and emotion
to what end remains unknown.

Arid apocalyptic dreams are useless
unless they are redeemed
by the all-embracing spirit
that suffuses everything
as an act of redemption.

Churches will fall empty.
Mosques will be home to birds.
Temples will fill with chattering apes,
Synagogues with sand and moaning winds.

Fossils of God
litter the world,
going under the burdens of time.

That God has passed this way,
dry records and crystalline rocks
carry the archaen testimony,
that certainty about God
is written in folly.

Burning obsidian and pumice spew out
From the liquid fire of heaving earth.
Animals eat, drink and live to be killed
As earth convulses in its act of birth.
The bones of neanders lie scattered about
Buried with the flinty tools they made,
Now fossils all. Wherever they fell they lay.
A gospel's getting wrenched out of rock and clay.
I see Ardi and Lucy look up at the sky,
I hear the god in them let out a cry
As they struggle with what they come to know,
Out of timelessness we come and go.

Never an ape, God, neither then nor now.
There's neither monkeys on Venus nor Mars.
We must keep re-defining what we know,
forsake the old creeds and look to the stars.
We all need to look for God where we live,
Where millions of years have come and gone,
In our skies, in our waters and in our land,
In our ever-evolving hearts and minds,
Look for his DNA in whatever we find,
His mystery for ever inviolate,
But approached as an act of faith.
I look at some pictures of Ardi's skull
From a distant six million years ago.
Through eye sockets light poured to bring in sight.
I wondered if ever there'd been a soul
In each of our ancestors who had passed this way.

If God is really in everything,
If God is really in each of us,
do we need to keep asking why he is.
Crying for his identity to be known?
Not to be human is not to be.
It leaves our arboreal identity in doubt,
About our evolving residential God
Who must have wondered what he was about,
Without language and reason to think it out.

Why, oh God, did it have to be this way,
Through timeless, cosmic dramas acted out
With big bangs and millions of suns and worlds
Till the time we arrived with all our doubts?

My God, if we didn't exist,
it would have left a dimension
of you unrealized and unfilled,
it would have left a part
of both of us unrealized.
Without us in you,
you would have remained
Coming into a Being
that would or could never
have been resolved.

And for all our coming into being,
as important as we may think it is,
we have played such an infinitely small part
of your Coming into Being,
so small that it hardly seems important at all,
that is if time is what we think it is,
time as a humanly discernible reality
to our tiny finite minds.

No one sees the seven colours of the rainbow
from the other side.
There is no other side.
The colours of the rainbow are meant for us
and it cannot abide
without the angle of the light
revealing it to us.

We build into it its myths and songs,
we hold it where it's meant to tell us
about your love,
your promise of life
after you had sent death into the world
and then, oh sad god,
you plastered a sad rainbow across the sky,
and we've never bothered asking why
sinner and sinless alike had to die.

Is that really all it is, complementarities,
life and death,
a balancing of yings and yangs?
Justice doesn't exist
in your cosmic scheme of things.
We can wring our hearts dry
of tears and fears
that came and went
in the blink of an eye,
but meant nothing to a heartless God.

In this fabric of stars, suns and galaxies
there will come a sad space,
of all who were born out of the storm
born out of the bio cosmic soup
lived, loved and died
and passed away,
victims of the grand eviction
as the new come into being as you.
Why did we have to know
the love and sadness that we found,
why the evil and the good?
Why were some forms of matter
flushed with soul?
How did matter find songs to sing
and re-create beauty in so many things
and all for so short a time?

Everything grows out of silence
Which is the nature of the void
In which resonance is felt
like language without words.
This is where beauty is born
And grows and waits for language
That has a kinship with you.

This is where we
who are born out of you
live for a while to affirm
your endless coming into being.

And I am left to ponder why
There are those who are born and die
Before the sun is set,
Others take too long
And cry out to die.
What has all this to do with you?

I think we who search for you
are lost in the labyrinth of many words
that keep changing
like the winds that blow;
we don't know from where they came
and where they go,
known only by what they make us feel,
known by what they do.
Sometimes there is a resonance
and sometimes there is danger

What is sacred is often lost to words
but are found between words,
concealed in between
and in the inexorable,
always bordering
on the unexpected and unknown,
waiting to be born,
to be given life anew,
concealed in the silences of time.

There was a time when
my thinking led me to believe
that all of life is a journey
begun at birth,
and ending in God,
but now I think that,
like all good pilgrims we were wrong.
Life cannot be a journey
if God is everywhere
and has always been,
without a beginning
and without an end
as an expression of advaita.

When I was a child I played like a child,
When I was a child I spoke like a child,
I learnt like a child all the things that
I carried into later life,
As I grew up I played like a child,
Often I was a sunbeam for the Lord,
I had learnt to pray like a child,
I had learnt the way to the church
and all the ways of the Church
and the creeds that had been around
for thousands of years killing me softly
and unobserved little by little,
it found me raging in anger against my God
and the deadness growing within.

As a child I learnt about the love of God
But I lived through a dozen savage wars and
Saw his love in burnt out cities
And the bodies of women and children
In smoldering remains of what were homes
Till I could no longer thank God for victories
Won on battlefields in his name.
Now I no longer play like a child
Nor do I think and act like a child.
I have seen how familiarity can serve
The blindfold of authority
With a happy servitude of a child.

Parched and barren
the Earth cries out for rain.
This happens only here on Earth
where you must also feel our pain
because it is yours as well, God of tears,
or are you also known to cry
on every planet in the galaxies,
for whatever crying happens to be?

You also feel the fear and pain
every mother feels as her infant
sucks its last desperately on empty tits,
and then it breathes its twitching last,
and in a shuddering, heartbreaking sigh
she knows she'll never again hear it cry.

As in childbirth pain comes with life anew
But I have great trouble getting the pictures
of babies and their mothers with
parchment and wrinkled skin,
bulging eyes and balloon-like bellies
gasping their last
making any difference to you.
Since all animal life has been in existence
these few million years past
it has been no different
in your coming into existence
as in evolutionary growth,
and it goes on and on.
What does it mean to you, our God?

What the world calls death
shapes our theologies
and keeps us shackled
to dualistic dreams of godhead.
They remain lost to the
luminosity of the Void
as they continue digging
old parched and dried up dreams
And wrap them up in creeds and dogmas.
My God, we continue to search
All that is without
for what can only be found within,
in you, oh God, for that is all there is,
the Beauty in Awesome Unity.

Do you hear them singing your praise
and invoking your help,
lost in worship and what passes for love
at the edges of the Abell
and the many other super novas?
What did you mean 13.7 billion years ago
and why should you mean today
what it is they say you mean to us?
I don't know why what men call the "Redeemer"
had to come when he did
in the "glorious, fullness" of time.
In the meeting place of the unknowns,
in the primordial depths of the Void,
are the startling truths that will be,
and whatever will be
are called into time and space.
Where are you in all this, oh God?
Everything and everyone who is born in you,
Grows in you, dies in you to grow in you
for whom there can be no death.

The Todd River was empty,
the watercourse was dry.
We climbed the rocks
to the top and saw
towering above us
the black shoulders
of Standly Chasm.

All around was still
but for the scuttling
of hidden life;
then the sun rose slowly
and tinged the shoulders of the chasm
towering like giants above us:
the darkness dissolved
into a startling pink that dripped
off the edges of the rockface
then slowly drenched the
entire chasm with
the deepest fiery red
that left the wall
in a sort of incandescent rage.

My senses lost themselves
In meaningless wilting reason,
And language lacked definition
And even today it has left me
nearly speechless;

had I been assaulted
by an epiphany
that rendered me helpless,
lost in time and space?

Just like as in today,
I find myself return
to that sacred hour,
grasping at echoes
and wondering why
the echoes come uncalled
searching for recognition
. . . and response?

Above me I still see
the eagles gracefully circling,
and I can still hear the scuttling
of hidden myriad of chasm life;
I still remember
the soft caressing summer breeze,
and me wondering
what it was all about.

Not every truth
lives to be understood.
Like yours mine calls
from another but distant part of me
that I cannot access but still I breathe in,
lost in wonder, love and grace.

Gautama had his Bodhi tree
under which he sat
and awoke to see that he
from the palace, pomp and power
had to set himself free
as he became lost in you, oh God,
as anyone must do
to respond to the power of epiphany.

In the world of desolation,
of burning sand and scrub,
Moses came by his burning bush
flames alive but without embers or ash,
and he removed his shoes
from off his feet
as the real world began to retreat.

Why do you need
your burning bushes and Bodhi trees,
Lascaux caves and Lourdes grottos?

Everywhere here on earth,
and out there on every planet, in every atom
and at the bottom of every sea
there should be an epiphany for all to see.

This life of ours is a life of spirit,
born into the numinous life
into the narrative of presence
which we sometimes and too often lose,
or worse still forget
and plunge into a life of guilt and regret.

Above me,
above Standly Chasm,
eagles hovered,
waiting for thermal currents
to help them on their way:
who knows when
or where the wind is born,
who knows where it will die?
So it is with every human being,
we are born out of chance
and, as we die in who or what we call God,
we finally release the burden of this life
with something like a gentle sigh.

Where ever we are
wherever we be,
cells die in us
cells come alive,
wherever we are, all around us
in all life forms,
animal, fish or fowl,
in viruses and bacteria
the drama never ends
in you and me,
anywhere, everywhere,
here on earth or
on the farthest stars,
in the ying and in the yang.

Wherever life is born
so soon it dies
so life can come again.
Galaxies explode and die.
In the outermost stretches of sky
galaxies are born.

God keeps coming into being
through death and life
and no language can ever
hope to tell it all.

From out of the black
of dark matter,
the blank of irreducible complexity,
that great big cloud of unknowing
and the singularities of science,
fly doubts that assail
at every hour, in every part
my meditative heart
that won't be still,
and I know that I ever will
still search for you,
and wonder how I belong
in all that is you
in everything and everywhere
that keeps racing away,
keeping on expanding,
but sending echoes back to us
in the unimagined and the unimaginable.

From the hypothetical point,
if ever there was one,
which never seems to have really been
without time and space,
a wonderful universe
has ever been latently alive.
From within this hypothetical point
you wished to be known
in those parts of you which became
cosmic time, in cosmic space,
in both matter and energy,
in your strange monologue.

Is any of this really so,
or is it what
we've been telling ourselves is so,
as you within yourself continue to grow?
It's your last chance to know yourself
in human terms of "human" being
as everything falls into
that ever widening maw
of the cold, ailing sun
to keep its weakening self alive,
as it desperately keeps swallowing all,
from whence came the myths of long ago
and has kept them alive all the while
and to what end only you would know.

Life hasn't always been
what it has evolved
from the past into today.
Why did it appear at all?
What isn't important to me
is how it all has come to be,
but why it has all happened so.

As once the burning orb
floated into its orbit
13.7 billion years ago
there were only fire and gas;
there was no death in the universe,
only life
being born
and everything that is
was taking shape
coming gradually into being.

Soulless matter began to stir
like a dream out of a distant sleep,
a sleep so profound,
where breathing laboured
and oceans and continents
tossed and heaved.
But where was fugitive soul
in all of this?
In such primal environment
of power and energy and little else?
The only language was
such power and energy,
unlettered in its own mystery.
Here was power without authority.

Some would have it
that in the beginning was the Word,
that mystical singularity
from which proceeded everything
with no answer to the Why?

Maybe that is a question
that cannot be asked;
Maybe that is a question
that needs no answers,
if such answers are never
meant to be understood,
but left to the silence of faith.

Planets revolve in their lonely galaxies
without any love or mercy,
where neither good nor bad,
without gospels or creeds
but only force and energy.
There nothing dies because nothing lives
not as we understand life.
Nothing breeds delusions and mythologies.
Only blind mountain ranges
and sterile lifeless plains—
and why should Earth have been meant
to be so different?

But here was where a mere handful of dirt
contained what became thoughts of you,
thoughts that dreamers pursued
ever since the dawn of ages;
here grew songs that were sung of you
as songs quivered from what climbed out
from the depths of the biological soup,
songs in search of singers of the ages.
Here were dreamers all intent on their truths
who wouldn't or couldn't stay silent
but wanted the world to know,
till things started to go horribly wrong
and where now hunger kills
and truth belongs only to the strong.

Here poets live to tell your tales, oh God,
dreams caught up in the echoes,
heard in dreams of you,
not without power
but without authority.

When I look into myself
I try to enter
where I fear to intrude
into where I have never been before,
I find only echoes from the past
whirling in some kaleidoscopic dance,
not unlike Plato's dancing shadows
in his cave-like self
and reality is expressed in metaphors.
Awareness lives a nano second life
that seeks definition and resolution
where there may well be none,
but only what was half begun.
We all identify with the intuitive life
of all things great and small.
I wonder if this is how
you came into being,
into what we call
time and space,
but I still don't know why.

There must have been more hidden
in black matter and black energy
before time and space.

I wonder if any theology
is or was aware of it,
and if it would have honestly
made any difference if it was.
Our world view is so limited
that we blindly snatch at fragments,
weave them into myths and metaphors
And claim that we know it all.

Billions of stars
and waterless planets
accelerate away from each other,
faster and faster,
and so will others not yet born.
Universes will explode into being
but not into life,
and where neither good and bad
will emerge from moral law
that will never exist
and you'll know no more
about yourself.
In that nano time and nano space
all will be forever gone
never to be found again
as had existed before
but in forms and accents unknown
and states yet unborn.

Other galaxies
in other universes
that existed once will be gone,
as the new ones
burst into being.
The time-honored questions
will never be asked again.
What we really were
we shall never know,
nor what we shall become,
become in awesome being
of advaita, the being of One.

Through out the other stretches
of worlds and universes
there are neither love nor hate,
and no such thing as sin;
no sin and moral systems.
It has been here only on earth
on one inconspicuous planet
of an obscure planetary system
that one called God came down
to save microbial-type beings
to give them eternal life.

This, after he missed out on a
few thousand years of earlier life,
and just why we do not know.
It is left as "in the fullness of time,"
whatever that may mean.
Why it happened in that one particular
corner of the world is not at all clear.
what a strange sort of choice
of time and space.
You have to wonder why,
and at what is called having faith.

I miss some hymns of old we used to sing.
We have no such songs but still we love to sing.
We lack the ritual dramas of long ago
that held those who still choose to sleep the sleep
in Sunday pews and mumble creeds
that drifted have down since the Nicene years
but now serve to feed their lazy ways.

Ours is the lonely and dry voice of reason
that others see as feckless treason
but we see as awakening from a sleep.
There's so much yet we have to learn
but we know that we shall never be sure
because all we have are questions
without answers, at least not yet.
I still sing those old songs whose echoes still
bring memories of what we once enjoyed
about what is remembered but not believed.

And are other worlds silent,
is there no music anywhere,
no one to sing-in eternal life
or is life not eternal in other worlds?
Astral winds fill the void
the wordless noise of empty spheres.
On earth it would have been the same,
a sad empty world without a name,
no mystery, no beauty, no songs to sing.
Why was earth ever so special
or is it our thinking that makes it so?
We are your self you can never know.

What if there had never been a big bang,
there could never have been an eternity.
We would never have found you, oh God
nor would you have come to know yourself
through us and through creation.

In the entire stretches of the cosmos
there is neither love nor hate,
no religions, no morals nor hate,
except down here on this lonely
and inconspicuous planet
tucked away on the outer fringe
of the Milky Way, equally irrelevant,
one of the smallest planetary systems
in the entirety of the universe.
Only here on this Earth
in Judea of ancient times
God came down to save
an elite microbial sort of world
after missing out a few
hundred thousand years that went before.
The other worlds didn't matter.
What a strange sort of choice
of time and place.
You have to wonder why
and what's this thing called faith.

Sing me the old, old story,
sing me the old, old story
the Allelujeh song of glory.

I miss the old songs
we used to sing,
songs I still sometimes sing
more for the memories
they always bring.
We lack the ritual dramas
of distant yesterdays
and which still hold
today's sleepers in their sleep
in Sunday pews mumbling creeds
that's drifted down from Nicean days
and thinking's lost in lazy ways.

Ours is the lonely voice of reason
that others see as feckless treason
but is really an awakening from a sleep.
There's so much more we have to learn,
but we know we can never be sure
because all we have are questions
but no answers, not as yet.
And so I shall sing those songs of old
and remember the stories I once was told
filled with memories of what I once enjoyed
but reason has since destroyed.

When I look into my inmost self
I seek to enter where I fear to tread,
I find echoes from past and present
swirling in kaleidoscopic dance,
something like Plato's dancing shadows
inside his cave-like self.
We are aware of so many fleeting things
but awareness lives a nanno life
that seeks definition and resolution
where there well may be none,
but only what was half begun.

We all seek this intuitive life
of all things great and small;
I wonder if this is how
we became aware of your being in us,
of you coming into being
into what we call
time and space.
I still don't know why you did.
This cannot be all.
There must be more
before
time and space.

You are the partner
of my solitude;
yours are the tears
that mix with mine.

You are the radiance in a smile
I beam into another's eyes
to bring another a moment's joy,
a resonance in each other's life.

You are my laughter
that wells up from inside,
that chases away doubts and fears
that sends the spirit dancing in the air.

You are my dance,
my exaltation,
my celebration
as we embrace,
which lets me feel
that I am in you
just as I feel you deep inside me.

Dance, sing and laugh.
We celebrate life
and the life in the hour
in the only way we can,
even if ever so briefly.

Mataranka goes on steaming
into the noontide light
that filters through the green canopy.
I am stilled and held breathless
as I stare into the ancient spring
where dragonflies dance about in ecstasy,
skimming the quietness that they bring.
Now is when I call to you my friend
to do something for the emptiness
that I know you find within me.

"I am what you are dreaming
at this ancient spring with its dragonflies
and the magical light that comes streaming.
Don't waken me yet, my God, my friend,
there's so much to do before the end."

There's a lot that's good
and happening at this very hour,
throughout the cosmos and in each of us.
Old stars die but new are born,
someone dies but another is born.
Something good keeps happening all the time.

I have come to paint the stars,
those old and sacred forms
fierce in all their splendor
that awakens in us this wonder
ever since it all began for us.

I have come to drink the wine
that pours out from dying worlds aflame
because I am made of longing
for their ecstasy to flood my veins
when I am alone with you.

I have come to dance
on the altars of the past.
I hear the choruses of empty songs.
Above them all I can hear the anthems
of new voices full of beauty and new hope.

We shall sing new hymns
you haven't heard before,
we shall make new wine
you haven't drunk before,
we shall paint new pictures
and life restore.

Renewal is born of honest faith.
The future was born a long time ago.

The clocks strikes the passing hour
and I cannot pretend any more
I haven't noticed how late it is.

Nothing is ever real to me
unless I bring it about.
Does that go for you, too?

If you don't shine the light within me,
the next time I look
I shall find it dark
with only echoes floating about.

When I turn the pages of
my photo album,
I find old letters, too,
telling me of the days that I have lived
but not always remembered—
you meant nothing to me then.
Did I mean anything to you?

When I put away my paints and brushes,
the picture isn't always complete.
Will all your universes ever be?
Will I find you
when all thinking ends?
Thinking cannot contain you,
who lives where nothing ends.

When the song that lifts me
above my doubts and fears ends
I will still be found singing
quietly to myself.

The six o'clock news shows us
faces and bellies distorted
by pain and hunger.
We know them as our brothers
who make the six o'clock news
just as we settle down to dinner.


You are our shepherd;
we are afraid to hear your call,
scared of what this might lead to,
what might lie ahead.
After all, the one who wandered off
might well be dead.


You see many in this world
who live as though
they've ceased to care,
or given up on you,
but you smile when you see
the anguish or surprise
on the faces of those who hunger
for your love,
and reveal yourself to you.

I am the world
God tumbled out of
in disarray,
confused in thought—
and started Coming into Being.


They veiled your face
from my waiting eyes
with all that solemn chanting,
wild tales
demanding my obedience
and my distance.


What the priests and prophets
mumbled as your name
remains a sacred mystery,
Nameless One.
What they've stammered and stuttered
about who you are
are secure in their creeds and dogmas,
and that gives them
the power without glory.

Our knowing is deeper
than our thoughts
that lie mired in
the daily round of common tasks
putting us beyond
the reach of ourselves.


I see in you
my mother's face,
her courage, love
and the fight to give us life
in a world from where love had fled.


I turn over to a new page
that is white with expectation
as it waits for whatever
will come to life.


A great presence stirring
beside me
claims my love and life,
but leaves me without
the will and strength
to be anything but what I am.

In silence
The Nameless One
draws near
and gently settles like a dream
and I am taken by surprise
and a tender fear.


I am made of flesh and blood,
limbs and bones,
arterial thoroughfares of pulsing life.
What I am made of
does not matter in this life:
I am made of longing.

Language isn't kind to you at all,
some say it makes you a cannibal,
because you eat human beings every day,
atheists, Buddhists, Muslims, Hindus and Jews,
we are all your breakfast, lunch and dinner,
regardless of whether you are good or a sinner.
This is my body given for you?
Do you reciprocate in this special way?
What is priceless is that you get to eat yourself
if it's true that we exist in you.

This is what we get for talking about you
as if you are a special sort of us
only writ large, but in a human sort of way.

It's equally silly for us to say
we are made in the image of you, oh God,
when we really have no idea in what way.
We don't know what we are talking about.

What do they call you out there on Mars
or even in those galaxies more afar,
many hundred billion kilometers away.
If there's no one there, do you go hungry?

Where are you, my God.
Tell me none of this is real
as we understand it.
Tell me again—
all we need is faith
that despite our unknowing
you are ever near at hand,
both in and without.

Suns,planets and worlds
race away from each other,
faster and faster still,
making our pixel earth
increasingly irrelevant,
last in its confusion and doubt.

What does this do for our consciousness?

Where are you, my God?
Tell us none of this is real
as we understand it.
Tell me again
despite our unknowing
you are ever near at hand
in us and without.